The Ultimate Book of
Netty Nutters

By the same author

Tarrant Off the Record: Tales from the Flip Side

The Ultimate Book of Netty Nutters

CHRIS TARRANT

Published in association with
Capital Radio and Help A London Child

HarperCollins*Entertainment*
An Imprint of HarperCollins*Publishers*

HarperCollins*Entertainment*
An imprint of HarperCollins*Publishers*
77–85 Fulham Palace Road,
Hammersmith, London W6 8JB
www.**fire**and**water**.com

A Paperback Original 1999
1 3 5 7 9 8 6 4 2

A catalogue record for this book is
available from the British Library

ISBN 0 00 653150 4

Set in Meridien

Printed and bound in Great Britain by
Caledonian International Book Manufacturing Ltd

FOREWORD

When everybody started raving about this thing called 'The Internet' a couple of years ago I had no idea what it was – and to a certain extent I still don't! But I have to say I was completely amazed by the way the whole thing took off so quickly. It has become a huge part of our daily lives and, like all new technology, you end up wondering how you ever coped without it.

For us on the Breakfast Show at 95.8 Capital FM it has opened up a whole new world of weird and wonderful things from around the globe. We get some brilliant e-mails over the internet from people listening to the Breakfast Show in bars, at work and even in bed at the end of the day, from places as far afield as Bahrain, the Caribbean, Australia and Hong Kong.

And then there's all the really silly stuff we get. Things You'll Never Hear A Man Say (like 'Aww, forget Match of the Day, let's watch a nice soppy film'; Questions (like 'Why don't psychics win the lottery?') and Bumper Stickers (like 'I didn't fight my way to the top of the food chain to become a vegetarian.')

It's all good fun and we get tons and tons of the stuff every day, but here is just a small selection that we thought you might enjoy. It certainly made us laugh!

FOOTBALL QUOTES

'I never make predictions, and I never will.'

Paul Gascoigne

'Beckenbauer really has gambled all his eggs.'

Ron Atkinson

'Celtic manager Davie Hay still has a fresh pair of legs up his sleeve.'

John Greig

'He's very fast and if he gets a yard ahead of himself nobody will catch him.'

Bobby Robson

'I can see the carrot at the end of the tunnel.'

Stuart Pearce

'The game is balanced in Arsenal's favour.'

John Motson

'A contract on a piece of paper, saying you want to leave, is like a piece of paper saying you want to leave.'

John Hollins

'What will you do when you leave football, Jack – will you stay in football?'

Stuart Hall

'Unfortunately, we keep kicking ourselves in the foot.'

Ray Wilkins

'I've got a gut feeling in my stomach …'

Alan Sugar

'I would not say he [David Ginola] is the best left winger in the Premiership, but there are none better.'

Ron Atkinson

'An inch or two either side of the post and that would have been a goal.'

Dave Bassett

'I never comment on referees and I'm not going to break the habit of a lifetime for that prat.'

Ron Atkinson

'The minute's silence was immaculate, I have never heard a minute's silence like that.'

Glenn Hoddle

'It's headed away by John Clark, using his head.'

Derek Rae

'What's it like being in Bethlehem, the place where Christmas began? I suppose it's like seeing Ian Wright at Arsenal ...'

Bruce Rioch

'If history is going to repeat itself, I should think we can expect the same thing again.'

Terry Venables

'You have got to miss them to score sometimes.'

Dave Bassett

'Dumbarton player Steve McCahill has limped off with a badly cut forehead.'

Tom Ferrie

'Bobby Robson must be thinking of throwing some fresh legs on.'

Kevin Keegan

'What makes this game so delightful is that when both teams get the ball they are attacking their opponents' goal.'

Jimmy Hill

'… and so they have not been able to improve their 100% record.'

Sports Roundup

'Certain people are for me and certain people are pro me.'

Terry Venables

Top 10 signs that the used car you bought is crap

1 You have to start warming it up before you go to bed at night.

2 The Dealer you bought it from wears a camel coat.

3 When you look under the bonnet, you find a hamster on a treadmill.

4 You keep getting pulled up by the police, who think you've just done a ram-raid.

5 The car's insurance is in group minus 5.

6 The salesman offers to throw in new car mats and mud-flaps before you even mentioned it.

7 As you drove off, you heard the salesman go … 'Du, du, du du … another one bites the dust!'

8 The small print of the owner's manual carries a government health warning.

9 Someone asks you how you managed to weld an Escort to a Clio.

10 The previous owner is registered as 'Trotter's Independent Trading'.

A dumb blonde went to a flight school insisting she wanted to learn to fly that day. As all the planes were currently in use, the owner agreed to instruct her on how to pilot a solo helicopter by radio. He took her out, showed her how to start it, gave her the basics, and set her on her way alone.

After she climbed 1,000 feet, she radioed in: 'I'm doing great! I love it! The view is so beautiful, and I'm starting to get the hang of this.'

After 2,000 feet, she radioed again, saying how easy it was becoming to fly. The instructor watched her climb over 3,000 feet, and was beginning to worry that she hadn't radioed in. A few minutes later, he watched in horror as she crashed about half a mile away. Luckily she was okay.

When he asked what happened, she said: 'I don't know! Everything was going fine, but as I got higher, I was starting to get cold. I can barely remember anything after I turned off the big fan.'

8 things you'll never hear a man say

8   Here, honey, you use the remote.

7   You know, I'd like to see her again, but her breasts are just too big.

6   Ooh, Antonio Banderas *and* Brad Pitt? That's one movie I gotta see!

5   While I'm up, can I get you anything?

4   Sex isn't that important, sometimes I just want to be held.

3   Aww, forget Match of the Day, let's watch a nice soppy film.

2   Hey, let me hold your coat while you try that on.

1   We never talk anymore.

8 things you'll never hear a woman say

8 What do you mean today's our anniversary?

7 Can we not talk to each other tonight. I'd rather just watch TV.

6 Ohh, this diamond is way too big!

5 Can our relationship get a little more physical? I'm tired of being 'just friends'.

4 Honey, does this outfit make my bum look too small?

3 Aww, don't stop for directions, I'm sure you'll be able to figure out how to get there.

2 I don't care if it's on sale, £250 is way too much for a designer dress.

1 Hey, pull my finger.

If other people played James Bond…

Ainsley Harriott stars as 007 in
'Can't Spy, Won't Spy'.

The Red Teletubby goes undercover in
'Dr Po'.

All Saints team up for
'Never Ever Say Never Ever Again'.

Tom Hanks is Bond in
'The Man With the Golden Gump'.

Paul Gasgoigne as 007 in
'Live and Eat Pies'.

A woman tells her friend that she's received a bunch of flowers from her husband. 'I suppose that I'll have to spend the whole weekend on my back with my legs in the air,' she says. Her friend replies: 'Why don't you just use a vase?'

Q What did the Spanish fireman call his two sons?
A Hose A and Hose B.

Microsoft's Bill Gates has said that if car technology had advanced at the same speed as computer technology, you'd now be able to drive around the world on a gallon of fuel. The chairman of General Motors hit back. He said that might be true, but your car would crash every four hours.

Bosses and employees

When I take a long time, I am slow.
When my boss takes a long time, he is thorough.

When I don't do it, I am lazy.
When my boss doesn't do it, he is too busy.

When I do something without being told, I am
trying to be smart.
When my boss does the same, that is initiative.

When I please my boss, I'm toadying.
When my boss pleases his boss, he's co-operating.

When I do good, my boss never remembers.
When I do wrong, he never forgets.

A JOB INTERVIEW

Young Dan Murphy applied for an engineering position at an Irish firm based in Dublin. An American applied for the same job and both applicants having the same qualifications were asked to take a test by the Department manager.

Upon completion of the test both men only missed one of the questions. The manager went to Murphy and said, 'Thank you for your interest, but we've decided to give the American the job.'

Murphy: 'And why would you be doing that? We both got 9 questions correct. This being Ireland and me being Irish I should get the job!'

Manager: 'We have made our decision – not on the correct answers, but on the question you missed.'

Murphy: 'And just how would one incorrect answer be better than the other?'

Manager: 'Simple. The American put down on question number 5 "I don't know." You put down "Neither do I"!'

They're not just pretty faces

'Mick Jagger and I just really liked each other a lot. We talked all night. We had the same views on nuclear disarmament.'

Jerry Hall

'They were doing a full back shot of me in a swimsuit and I thought, Oh my God, I have to be so brave. See every woman hates herself from behind.'

Cindy Crawford

'I can do anything you want me to do so long as I don't have to speak.'

Linda Evangelista

I'm not saying that my wife over-extends our credit, but her Visa card has a racing stripe on it.

Yesterday scientists in the USA revealed that beer contains small traces of female hormones. To prove their theory they fed 100 men 12 pints of beer and observed that 100% of them started talking nonsense and couldn't drive ...

Wife: 'Let's go out and have some fun tonight.'
Husband: 'Okay. But if you get home before I do, leave the hallway light on.'

If your wife and a lawyer were drowning and you had to choose what to do, would you go to lunch or to a movie?

Thoughts for the day

Before they invented drawing boards,
what did they go back to?

If love is blind, why is lingerie
so popular?

Do infants enjoy infancy as much as adults enjoy adultery?

How is it possible to have a civil war?

If work is so terrific, how come they have to pay you to do it?

If you try to fail, and succeed, which have you done?

If a mute swears, does his mother wash his hands with soap?

Why don't psychics win the lottery?

A guy walks into a pub, walks up to the bar, and the landlord asks him what he wants. The man says, 'I'll have a pint of lager, please.' The landlord pulls him a pint and says, 'That will be £2, please.' The bloke says, 'No, you asked me what I wanted and I said a pint and you gave it me, so I don't have to pay' The landlord says, 'Well, you can drink your pint but then clear off.'

Two weeks later, the same bloke walks into the same pub and asks for a pint of lager. The landlord says, 'I remember you. You tried this trick two weeks ago.' The guy says, 'No, I didn't.' The Landlord says, 'Well then you must have a double.' Bloke replies, 'Okay then, make it a whiskey!'

CRAZY SIGNS
How do they expect to sell these?

Dinner Special – Turkey £2.35,
Chicken or Beef £2.25, Children £2.

Mixing Bowl set for sale: have round
bottoms for efficient beating.

For sale: antique dresser suitable for lady
with thick legs and large drawers.

Now is your chance to get your ears pierced
and take home an extra pair too.

We do not tear your clothing with machinery.
We do it carefully by hand.

God decides enough is enough and decides to end the world. In order to give some notice of this he summons Bill Clinton, Boris Yeltsin and Bill Gates to His presence, and tells them the world will end the following day.

When he gets home, Bill Clinton calls his advisors and says, 'I've got some good news and some bad news. The good news is that God exists, the bad news is that the world will end tomorrow.'

Boris Yeltsin gets back and calls his advisors together and says, 'I've some bad news and some really bad news. The bad news is that God exists, and the really bad news is that the world will end tomorrow.'

Bill Gates gets back and says to his top managers, 'I've some great news and some really great news. The great news is that God thinks I'm one of the top most three important people in the world. The really great news is that we don't have to worry about sorting out the bugs in Windows 95.'

Questions about love and marriage were posed to kids aged 5 to 10 from a junior school in Philadelphia ...

What is the proper age to get married?
Eighty-four, because at that age you don't have to work anymore and you can spend all your time loving each other in your bedroom. (Judy, 8)

What do most people do on a date?
On the first date they just tell each other lies, and that usually gets them interested enough to go for a second date. (Mike, 10)

When is it okay to kiss someone?
You should never kiss a girl unless you have enough bucks to buy her a big ring and her own VCR, 'cause she'll want to have videos of the wedding. (Jim, 10)

It's never okay to kiss a boy. They always slobber all over you ... that's why I stopped doing it. (Jean, 10)

The great debate: is it better to be single or married?
It's better for girls to be single but not for boys. Boys need somebody to clean up after them. (Lynette, 9)

Concerning why love happens between two particular people
No one is sure why it happens, but I heard it has
something to do with how you smell. That's why
perfume and deodorant are so popular. (Jan, 9)

On what falling in love is like
Like an avalanche where you have to run for your
life. (Roger, 9)

If falling in love is anything like learning how to spell,
I don't want to do it. It takes too long. (Leo, 7)

Confidential opinions about love
I'm in favour of love as long as it doesn't happen
when 'The Simpsons' is on television. (Anita, 6)

The personal qualities necessary to be a good lover
One of you should know how to write a cheque.
Because, even if you have tons of love, there is still
going to be a lot of bills. (Ava, 8)

Some sure-fire ways to make a person fall in love with you
Tell them that you own a whole bunch of candy
stores. (Del, 6)

Don't do things like have smelly, green sneakers. You
·might get attention, but attention ain't the same thing
as love. (Alonzo, 9)

One way is to take the girl out to eat. Make sure it's something she likes to eat. French fries usually works for me. (Bart, 9)

How can you tell if two adults eating dinner at a restaurant are in love?
Lovers will just be staring at each other and their food will get cold. Other people care more about the food. (Brad, 8)

It's love if they order one of those desserts that are on fire. They like to order those because it's just like how their hearts are ... on fire. (Christine, 9)

What most people are thinking when they say 'I love you'
The person is thinking: Yeah, I really do love him. But I hope he showers at least once a day. (Michelle, 9)

How a person learns to kiss
You learn it right on the spot when the gooshy feelings get the best of you. (Doug, 7)

It might help to watch soap operas all day. (Carin, 9)

How often do you clean your bathroom? Bathroom cleanliness is so important to 26% of adults that they clean the bath after every use. Older people are considerably more likely to be this fussy. Almost half of those 65 and older clean the bath every time. At the other extreme, 8% of us clean the bath less than once a month ... or not at all!

Dilbert's laws of work

If you can't get your work done in the first
24 hours, work nights.

A pat on the back is only a few centimetres
from a kick in the butt.

There will always be beer cans on the floor of
your car when your boss asks for a ride home
from the office.

Never delay the ending of a meeting or the
beginning of happy hour.

If you are good, you will be assigned all of the work.
If you are really good, you will get out of it.

If it wasn't for the last minute, nothing would
ever get done.

A man walks into a pub and gets a drink. The pub is very busy and there's only one place to sit, at a table where someone is already sitting. The first guy asks if it's all right to sit down and the other guy says, 'Sure.'

'Great,' says the first guy, 'but I insist I buy you a drink.' Which he does, then the second guy buys a round, and very soon they're both pretty far gone. When the bell goes, the second guy says, 'Have you got a car?'

'Sure,' says the first guy, 'it's outside.'
'OK, we'll drive back to your place and have a nightcap.'

As they both get up to leave, the second guy falls flat on his face and knocks out his front teeth. He staggers up but falls straight over again and splits his head open on the bar.

The first guy helps him up and points him towards the door but he falls forward again and puts his head through the pub glass door. With that the first guy helps him to his car but he falls flat on his face again getting into the car.

'Look,' says the first guy, 'you're too plastered. I'll just drop you off at your house and we'll call it a night.'

'OK, you're right,' agrees the second guy. So the first guy drops him off at his front door. Next morning he wakes up covered in dried blood, his face a mass of bruises, his teeth missing and generally in a lot of pain.

'Jeez, I was drunk last night,' he says to his wife.

'Drunk?' she says. 'Drunk? You were so drunk, you forgot your wheelchair.'

I'm a bit concerned by the number of low fat spreads which make claims that you can't tell them from real butter. There's 'I Can't Believe It's Not Butter', 'You'd Butter Believe It', 'Utterly Butterly' and a thousand more. My worry is that after a certain time children who've been brought up on these spreads won't know what it was that they don't know they're not having.

One night there are three Essex girls walking home .. and the first shouts out, 'Look here, some rabbit tracks!' The second girl says, 'Don't be stupid, they're badger tracks.' The third girl comes over and is just about to say 'They're fox tracks,' when a train runs all three of them over.

From actual letters sent to the DHSS ...

In reply to your letter, I have already cohabited with your officer with no results so far.

I am pleased to inform you that my husband who was reported missing, is dead.

Unless I get my husband's maintenance money soon I shall be obliged to live an immortal life.

You have changed my little boy into a little girl? Will this matter?

Mrs Brown only *thinks* she's ill, but believe me she is nothing but a hypodermic.

In accordance with your instructions, I have given birth to twins in the enclosed envelope.

Some useful descriptions of people you may work with

He's not the sharpest knife in the drawer.

He's got a room temperature IQ.

He's about as bright as Alaska in December.

If brains were taxed, he'd get a rebate.

If he were any more stupid, he'd have to be watered once a week.

Q What's the difference between snowmen and snow women?
A Snowballs.

Q What do you call a man with a raincoat on his head?
A Mack

Q What do you call a man with two raincoats on his head?
A Max

Q What do you call a man with two raincoats on his head sitting in a cemetery?
A Max Bygraves.

PHONEY NEWSPAPER HEADLINES

Shrewsbury Star
'Trouble at balloon factory blown out of all proportion.'

Salisbury Echo
'Stonehenge to host ROCK concert.'

Banbury Echo
'Vicar to give his car a service.'

Newcastle Courier
'Man back late from coffee break really takes the biscuit.'

Alabama Journal
'Native Americans putting on a brave face.'

Swindon Guardian
'Press statement from asylum is just crazy talk.'

Warning labels

A 'Wacky Warning Label Contest' in America has announced its winners. In reverse order: 'Never use hair dryer while sleeping', from a hair dryer. 'Do not drive with sunshield in place', from a windshield sunscreen. And the winner … 'Caution: Do not spray in eyes', from a spray deodorant can.

A top 5 of things you don't want to hear on your Honeymoon night

5 I can't wait 'til this whole ordeal is over so I can get back to cruising the singles' bars again.

4 Let's make this fast. I want to be home for the match.

3 There's no rush. But, just so you know, we're paying for this room by the hour.

2 I can't wait to introduce you to the rest of my friends in the William Hague Fan Club.

1 What's your name again?

Actual true stories told by Travel Agents

✈ One customer asked for an aisle seat – so that her hair wouldn't get messed up by being near the window!

✈ A man called, furious about a Florida package we did. I asked what was wrong with the vacation in Orlando. He said he was expecting an ocean-view room. I tried to explain that that is not possible, since Orlando is in the middle of the state. He replied, 'Don't lie to me; I looked on the map and Florida is a very thin state.'

✈ A nice lady just called. She needed to know how it was possible that her flight from Detroit left at 8.30 a.m. and got into Chicago at 8.33 a.m. I tried to explain that Michigan was an hour ahead of Illinois, but she could not understand the concept of time zones. Finally I told her the plane went very fast, and she bought that!

✈ I just got off the phone with a man who asked, 'How do I know which plane to get on?' I asked him what exactly he meant, to which he replied, 'I was told my flight number is 823, but none of the planes have numbers on them.'

✈ A businessman called and had a question about the documents he needed in order to fly to China. After a lengthy discussion about passports, I reminded him he needed a visa. 'Oh no I don't. I've been to China many times and they have always accepted my American Express.'

✈ I got a call from a woman who wanted to go to Capetown. I started to explain the length of the flight and the passport information when she interrupted me with, 'I'm not trying to make you look stupid, but Capetown is in Massachusetts.' Without trying to make *her* look like the stupid one, I calmly explained, 'Cape Cod is in Massachusetts, Capetown is in Africa.' She put the phone down on me.

A woman called to make reservations. 'I want to go from Chicago to Hippopotamus, New York.' The agent was at a loss for words. Finally, the agent said, 'Are you sure that's the name of the town?' 'Yes. What flights do you have?' replied the customer. After some searching, the agent came back with, 'I'm sorry, ma'am, I've looked up every airport code in the country and can't find a Hippopotamus anywhere.' The customer retorted, 'Oh don't be silly. Everyone knows where it is. Check your map!' The agent scoured a map of the state of New York and finally offered, 'You don't mean Buffalo, do you?' 'That's it! I knew it was a big animal!'

Signs translated to English around the world

In a Yugoslavian hotel
'The flattening of underwear with pleasure is the job of the chambermaid.'

In an Acapulco hotel
'The manager has personally passed all the water served here.'

In a Bucharest hotel
'The lift is being fixed for the next day. During that time we regret that you will be unbearable.'

In a hotel in Athens
'Visitors are expected to complain at the office between the hours of 9 and 11 a.m. only.'

On the menu of a Swiss restaurant
'Our wines leave you nothing to hope for.'

In a Hong Kong supermarket
'For your convenience, we recommend courageous, efficient self-service.'

In a Bangkok dry cleaners
'Drop your trousers here for best results.'

In a Rome laundry
'Ladies, leave your clothes here and spend the afternoon having a good time.'

Advertisement for donkey rides in Thailand
'Would you like to ride on your own ass?'

In a Tokyo bar
'Special cocktails for the ladies with nuts.'

In a Leipzig elevator
'Do not enter the lift backwards, and only when lit up.'

Outside a Paris dress shop
'Dresses for street walking.'

Q What do you call a man that sits at the front or back of a car?
A Reg.

Q What does his brother call him?
A R Reg.

Q What do you call him when he's dead?
A X Reg.

**Did you hear the one about the dyslexic pimp?
He bought himself a warehouse!**

'I've just spent a Christmas from hell. My kids woke me up at 5 a.m. on Christmas Day demanding their presents, wouldn't eat their sprouts and then cried all the way through the Queen's Speech. I tell you, I'd give them hell if I didn't know they'll be the ones who eventually choose my Old People's Home.'

Things that make you go Hhhmmm ...

Where is the skin of your teeth?

Are thieves really thick?

How do you go bananas?

How cheap is dirt?

What does a pretty pickle look like?

LAWYER JOKES

What's the difference between a lawyer and a leech?
A leech quits sucking your blood after you die.

Why did God invent lawyers?
So that estate agents would have someone to look down on.

What's the difference between a lawyer and a trampoline?
You would take your shoes off to jump on a trampoline.

Q How do you make an Irishman burn his ear?
A Phone him while he's ironing.

A little turtle begins to climb a tree slowly. After long hours of effort, he reaches the top, jumps into the air waving his front legs, until he falls heavily on to the ground with a hard knock on his shell. After recovering consciousness, he starts to climb the tree slowly again, jumps again, and falls heavily on to the ground once more. The little turtle picks himself up, and begins to climb the tree again. A couple of birds, sitting at the edge of a branch, look at the turtle with pain. Suddenly the female bird says to the male: 'Hey, dear, I think it's time to tell our little turtle he's adopted.'

BUMPER STICKERS

The best way to a man's heart is to saw
his breast plate open.

Don't trust anything that bleeds for 5 days
and doesn't die.

Beauty is only a light switch away.

I've decided that to raise my grades I must
lower my standards.

God made pot. Man made beer. Who do you trust?

Fighting for peace is like screwing for virginity.

No matter how good she looks, some other guy is
sick and tired of putting up with her crap.

It's hard to make a comeback when you
haven't been anywhere.

If voting could really change things,
it would be illegal.

JESUS SAVES!
But wouldn't it be better if he had invested?

FACTS

In an average lifetime we spend nine-and-a half days putting our undies on.

Digestive biscuits were invented to control flatulence.

Women who are on the Pill blink an average 33% more than women who aren't.

We all have a 1 in 5,000 chance of dying from flu.

60% of smokers want to give up.

Some people are born losers ...

★ In 1992, Frank Perkins of Los Angeles made an attempt on the world flagpole-sitting record. By the time he came down, finally, his sponsor had gone bust, his girlfriend had left him, his phone and electricity had been cut off – and he was still eight hours short of the 400-day record.

★ The average cost of rehabilitating a seal after the Exxon Valdez oil spill in Alaska was $80,000. At a special ceremony, two of the most expensively saved animals were released back into the wild amid cheers and applause from onlookers. A minute later they were both eaten by a killer whale.

★ Two animal rights protesters were protesting at the cruelty of sending pigs to a slaughter house in Bonn. Suddenly the pigs, all two thousand of them, escaped through a broken fence and stampeded, trampling the two hapless protesters to death.

★ A fierce gust of wind blew 45-year-old Vittorio Luise's car into a river near Naples, Italy in 1983. He managed to break a window, climb out, and swim to shore – where a tree blew over and killed him.

★ George Schwartz, owner of a factory in Providence, R. I., narrowly escaped death when a 1983 blast flattened his factory except for one wall. After treatment for minor injuries, he returned to the scene to search for his files. The remaining wall then collapsed on him, killing him instantly.

★ In 1983, a Mrs Carson of Lake Kushaqua, N.Y. was laid out in her coffin, presumed dead of heart disease. As mourners watched, she suddenly sat up. Her daughter dropped dead of fright.

★ A man hit by a car in New York City in 1977 got up uninjured, but lay back down in front of the car when a bystander told him to pretend he was hurt so that he could collect insurance money. The car then rolled forward and crushed him to death.

★ Iraqi terrorist, Khay Rahnajet, didn't pay enough postage on a letter bomb. It came back with 'Return to Sender' stamped on it. He opened it and said a fond farewell to his face.

★ Surprised while burgling a house in Antwerp, Belgium, a thief fled out the back door, clambered over a nine-foot wall and dropped straight into the city prison.

★ Two German motorists had a head-on collision in heavy fog near the small town of Guetersloh – literally! Each was guiding his car at a snail's pace from opposite directions but both near the middle of the road. At the moment of impact, their heads were both out of the windows, where they smacked together. Both men were hospitalized with head injuries. Their cars were unscratched.

Recently reported in the Massachusetts Bar Association Lawyers Journal, the following are questions actually asked of witnesses by attorneys during trials:

'Were you present when your picture was taken?'

'Were you alone or by yourself?'

'Did he kill you?'

Q 'All your responses must be oral, okay? What school did you go to?'
A 'Oral.'

'Was it you or your younger brother who was killed in the war?'

Q 'Doctor, how many autopsies have you performed on dead people?'
A '*All* my autopsies have been performed on dead people.'

Q 'You said the stairs went down to the basement?'
A 'Yes.'
Q 'And these stairs, did they go up also?'

Q 'Can you describe the individual?'
A 'He was about medium height and had a beard.'
Q 'Was this a male, or a female?'

Q 'You were not shot in the fracas?'
A 'No, I was shot midway between the fracas and the navel.'

'How many times have you committed suicide?'

Things we have learned from the movies

All beds have special L-shaped top sheets which reach up to armpit level on a woman but only to waist level on the man lying beside her.

Large, loft-style apartments in New York City are well within the price range of most people – whether they are employed or not.

Even when driving down a perfectly straight road it is necessary to turn the steering wheel vigorously from left to right every few moments.

At least one of a pair of identical twins is born evil.

A detective can only solve a case once he has been suspended from duty.

If you decide to start dancing in the street everyone you bump into will know all the steps.

Should you decide to defuse a bomb, don't worry which wire to cut. You will always choose the right one.

Most laptop computers are powerful enough to override the communications system of any invading alien society.

It does not matter if you are heavily outnumbered in a fight involving martial arts – your enemies will wait patiently to attack you one by one by dancing around in a threatening manner until you have knocked out their predecessors.

When you turn out the light to go to bed, everything in your bedroom will still be clearly visible, just slightly bluish.

When paying for a taxi, the actors never look at their wallet as they take out a note – just grabbing one at random and handing it over. It will always be the exact fare.

The Eiffel Tower can be seen from any window in Paris.

The man never has to dispose of any contraceptive device after bedroom scenes.

If staying in a haunted house, women always investigate any strange noises in their most revealing underwear.

All shopping bags contain at least one stick of French bread.

It's easy for anyone to land a plane provided there's someone in the control tower to talk them down.

Once applied, lipstick will never rub off … even if the star is hospitalized … the patient will always manage to have the lipstick on days later.

The ventilation system of any building is the perfect hiding place. No one will ever think of looking for them in there and they can travel to any other part of the building they want … no problem!

A man will show no pain while taking the most ferocious beating but will wince when a woman tries to clean his wounds.

Kitchens don't have light switches. When entering a kitchen at night, actors simply open the fridge door and use that light instead.

Any person waking from a nightmare will sit bolt upright and pant.

It's always possible to park directly outside the building you're visiting.

You never see horse manure on the dusty streets in Westerns.

A man was hassling an airline agent at the ticket counter – yelling, using foul language, etc. The agent remained calm, polite, pleasant and smiled throughout the harangue.

When the man finally left, the next person in the queue said to the agent, 'Does that happen often? I can't believe how nice you were to him.'

The agent smiled and said, 'It's easy. I've booked him on a flight to Paris – and his bags are on a flight to Japan!'

Actual sentences found in church notices and newsletters

This afternoon there will be a meeting in the south and north ends of the church. Children will be baptized at both ends.

For those of you who have children and don't know it, we have a nursery downstairs.

Weight Watchers will meet at 7.00 p.m. at the Presbyterian church. Please use large double door at side entrance.

Eight new choir robes are currently needed, due to the addition of several new members and the deterioration of some older ones.

Don't let worry kill you. Let the church help.

At the evening service tonight, the sermon topic will be 'What is Hell?' Come early and listen to the choir practice.

The Associate Minister unveiled the church's new tithing campaign slogan last Sunday: 'I Upped My Pledge – Up Yours.'

STUPID LOCAL LAWS

✗ In Pennsylvania it is illegal to have over 16 women living in a house together because that constitutes a brothel. However, up to 120 men can live together without breaking the law.

✗ In New York it is against the law to throw a ball at someone's head for fun.

✗ The state of Washington has passed a law stating that it is illegal to paint polka dots on the American flag.

✗ For a pickle to be officially considered a pickle in Connecticut, it must bounce.

✗ In Manville, N.J. it is illegal to feed whiskey or offer cigarettes to animals at the local zoo. It is also forbidden for a person to take a bite out of another person's hamburger.

✗ In the state of New York, you need a licence to use a clothesline outdoors.

✘ In Ottumwa, Iowa, 'It is unlawful for any male person, within the corporate limits of the city, to wink at any female person with whom he is unacquainted.'

✘ In Los Angeles, you cannot bathe two babies in the same tub at the same time.

✘ In Carmel, N.Y. a man can't go outside while wearing a jacket and trousers that do not match.

✘ In Hartford, Connecticut, you aren't allowed to cross a street while walking on your hands.

✘ In Baltimore, it is illegal to throw bales of hay from a second-storey window within the city limits. It's also illegal to take a lion to the movies.

✘ In Oxford, Ohio, it is illegal for a woman to strip off her clothing while standing in front of a picture of a man.

Suggested titles for new movies about the Clinton administration

Citizen Stain

Saving Clinton's Privates

All the President's Women

The Lying King

The Full Monica

Terms of Impeachment

Neither an Officer Nor a Gentleman

Women's words of wisdom

'I'm not offended by all the dumb blonde jokes because I know I'm not dumb … and I also know that I'm not blonde.'

Dolly Parton

'I figure that if the children are alive when he gets home, I've done my job.'

Roseanne

'In politics, if you want anything said, ask a man; if you want anything done, ask a woman.'

Margaret Thatcher

'Sometimes I wonder if men and women really suit each other. Perhaps they should live next door and just visit now and then.'

Katharine Hepburn

'I am a marvellous housekeeper. Every time I leave a man I keep his house.'

Zsa Zsa Gabor

'I'm not going to vacuum 'til they make one you can ride on.'

Roseanne

'I would love to speak a foreign language, but I can't. So I grew hair under my arms instead.'

Sue Kolinsky

'I think – therefore I'm single.'

Lizz Winstead

'I base most of my fashion taste on what doesn't itch.'

Gilda Radner

'Behind every successful man is a surprised woman.'

Maryon Pearson

'I have yet to hear a man ask for advice on how to combine marriage and a career.'

Gloria Steinem

'I never married because there was no need. I have three pets at home which serve the same purpose as a husband. I have a dog which growls every morning, a parrot which swears all afternoon and a cat that comes home late at night.'

Marie Corelli

'If men can run the world, why can't they stop wearing neckties? How intelligent is it to start the day by tying a little noose around your neck?'

Linda Ellerbee

AMAZING
HUMAN FACTS

If you yelled for eight years, seven months and
six days, you would have produced enough
sound energy to heat one cup of coffee.

Banging your head against a wall uses
150 calories an hour.

KINETIC
AEROBICS

LOSE
WEIGHT
FAST!

The human heart creates enough pressure
when it pumps out to the body to squirt
blood thirty feet.

Humans and dolphins are the only species
that have sex for pleasure.

On average, people fear spiders more than
they do death.

The strongest muscle in the body is the tongue.

It's impossible to sneeze with your eyes open.

You can't kill yourself by holding your breath.

Did you know that you are more likely to
be killed by a champagne cork than by a
poisonous spider?

Right-handed people live, on average,
nine years longer than left-handed people.

In ancient Egypt, priests plucked every hair
from their bodies, including their eyebrows
and eyelashes.

AMAZING
ANIMAL FACTS

A crocodile cannot stick its tongue out.

Polar bears are left handed.

A cockroach will live nine days without its
head before it starves to death.

Some lions mate over fifty times a day.

Butterflies taste with their feet.

Starfish haven't got brains.

Three friends die in a car crash. They go to an orientation class in Heaven.

During the class, they are all asked, 'When you are in your coffin and friends and family are mourning you, what would you like to hear them say about you?'

The first guy says, 'I would like to hear them say that I was a great doctor of my time and a great family man.'

The second guy says, 'I would like to hear that I was a wonderful husband and school teacher, who made a huge difference to the children of tomorrow.'

The last guy replies, 'I would like to hear them say *"Look, he's moving!"'*

You're probably aged 25–35 if …

✳ You wore a Kagool that folded up into a pouch you could wear around your waist.

✳ You remember when there was no breakfast TV and when TV shut down at midnight.

✳ You remember when leg warmers were cool.

✳ Bo, Luke and Daisy Duke are fond memories.

✳ There was nothing strange about Bert 'n' Ernie living together in Sesame Street.

✳ You know who shot J.R.

✳ This rings a bell: 'My name is Charlie. They work for me.'

It's not the pace of life that concerns me;
   it's the sudden stop at the end.

If God wanted me to touch my toes,
he would have put them on my knees.

Never knock on Death's door.
Ring the doorbell and run.

Lead me not into temptation.
I can find the way myself.

The mind is like a parachute;
it works much better when it's open.

Never take life seriously.
Nobody gets out alive, anyway.

Genuine extracts from letters sent to the Council

'This is to let you know that our lavatory seat is broken and we cannot get BBC.'

'I wish to complain that my father hurt his ankle very badly when he put his foot in the hole in his back passage.'

'The lavatory is blocked. This is caused by the boys next door throwing their balls on the roof.'

'This is to let you know that there is a smell coming from the man next door.'

'The toilet seat is cracked, where do I stand?'

'I request your permission to remove my drawers in the kitchen.'

'Our lavatory seat has broken in half and is now in three pieces.'

'Can you please tell me when our repairs are going to be done as my wife is about to become an expectant mother.'

'I want some repairs doing to my cooker as it has backfired and burnt my knob off.'

'The toilet is blocked and we cannot bath the children until it is cleared.'

'The person next door has a large erection in his back garden, which is unsightly and dangerous.'

'Will you please send someone to mend our broken path. Yesterday my wife tripped on it and is now pregnant.'

'Our kitchen is very damp. We have two children and would like a third, so will you please send someone to do something about it.'

'When I applied for a rebate you said that you would have to take something off. Now that you have taken it off, I have been told that you should have put some on. So will you please take off what you took off and put on what you should have put on when you took it off.'

The experts speak

'This "telephone" has too many shortcomings to be seriously considered as a means of communication. The device is inherently of no value to us.'

Western Union internal memo, 1876

'Computers in the future may weigh no more than 1.5 tons.'

Popular Mechanics, forecasting the relentless march of science, 1949

'640k ought to be enough for anybody.'

Bill Gates, 1981

'There is no reason why anyone would want a computer in their home ...'

Ken Olson, president, chairman and founder of Digital Equipment

In a laundry room
'Do not put wet clothes in dryer, as this can cause irreparable damage.'

In a New York restaurant
'Customers who find our waitresses rude ought to see the manager.'

In the window of an Oregon general store
'Why go elsewhere to be cheated, when you can come here?'

In a Pennsylvanian cemetery
'Persons are prohibited from picking flowers from any but their own graves.'

On a Tennessee highway
'Take notice: when this sign is under water, this road is impassable.'

If Men Got Pregnant ...

Maternity leave would last for two years
... with full pay.

There would be a cure for stretch marks.

Natural childbirth would become obsolete.

Morning sickness would rank as the
nation's number one health problem.

All methods of birth control would be
100% effective.

They wouldn't think twins were so cute.

Sons would have to be home from dates
by 10 p.m.

Some thoughts ...

☆ When everything's coming your way, you're in the wrong lane.

☆ I drive way too fast to worry about cholesterol.

☆ What happens if you get scared half to death twice?

☆ I intend to live for ever – so far, so good.

☆ Shin: a device for finding furniture in the dark.

☆ The only substitute for good manners is fast reflexes.

☆ Beauty is in the eye of the beer holder ...

☆ When I'm not in my right mind, my left mind gets pretty crowded.

☆ Everyone has a photographic memory. Some don't have film.

☆ Dancing is a perpendicular expression of a horizontal desire ...

A list of 'code words' in the Lonely Hearts ads

MALE PROFILE WORDS

40-ish	52 and looking for 25-year-old
Affectionate	Needy and looking for mother figure
Artist	Delicate ego badly in need of massage
Athletic	Sits on the sofa watching football
Average looking	Unusual hair growth on ears, nose and back
Distinguished looking	Fat, grey and bald
Friendship first	As long as friendship involves nudity
Fun	Good with a remote control and a six-pack
Good looking	Arrogant pig
Honest	Pathological liar
Huggable	Overweight, more body hair than King Kong
Light drinker	Headed for AA
Mature	Until you get to know him
Open-minded	Wants to sleep with your sister
Thoughtful	Says 'please' when demanding a beer

Letters of complaint

'Will you please send a man to look at my water. It is a funny colour and not fit to drink.'

'Could you please send someone to fix our bath tap. My wife got her toe stuck in it and it was very uncomfortable for us.'

'When the workmen were here they put their tools in my wife's new drawers and made a mess. Please send men with clean tools to finish the job and keep my wife happy.'

'I want to complain about the farmer across the road. Every morning his cock wakes me up, and it is getting too much.'

Five reasons to believe computers are female

1 No one but the Creator understands their internal logic.

2 The native language they use to communicate with other computers is incomprehensible to everyone else.

3 The message 'Bad command or file' is about as informative as 'If you don't know why I'm mad at you, then I'm certainly not going to tell you.'

4 Even your smallest mistakes are stored in long-term memory for later retrieval.

5 As soon as you make a commitment to one, you find yourself spending half your paycheque on accessories for it.

Five reasons to believe computers are male

1 They have a lot of data, but are still clueless.

2 They are supposed to help you solve problems, but half the time they *are* the problem.

3 As soon as you commit to one you realize that, if you had waited a little longer, you could have obtained a better model.

4 In order to get their attention, you have to turn them on.

5 Big power surges knock them out for the rest of the night.

Things to ponder

Why do you press harder on a remote control
when you know the batteries are dead?

Light travels faster than sound ... isn't that
why some people appear bright until you
hear them speak?

Why are they called buildings when they're
already finished? Shouldn't they be
called 'builts'?

Why is a carrot more orange than an orange?

Why is it, when a door is open it's ajar,
but when a jar is open it's not a door?

ADVERTISEMENTS

Illiterate? Write today for free advice.

Auto Repair Service: Try us once, you'll never go anywhere else again.

Dog for sale: Eats anything, loves children.

Girl wanted to assist magician in cutting off head illusion: Medical insurance and salary included.

Something to think about

Coca-Cola was originally green.

It is possible to lead a cow upstairs but not downstairs.

Men can read smaller print than women; women can hear better.

The amount that American Airlines saved in 1987 by eliminating one olive from each salad served in first class was … $40,000!

Average number of days a West German used to go without washing his underwear: seven.

Percentage of American men who say they would marry the same woman if they had to do it all over again: 80%. Percentage of American women who say they'd marry the same man: 50%.

Intelligent people have more zinc and copper in their hair.

First novel ever written on a typewriter: *Tom Sawyer*.

The name Wendy was made up for the book *Peter Pan*.

Average number of people airborne over the US any given hour: 61,000.

Modern philosophies

If at first you don't succeed, destroy all evidence that you tried.

A conclusion is the place where you got tired of thinking.

Experience is something you don't get until just after you need it.

For every action, there is an equal and opposite criticism.

He who hesitates is probably right.

Success always occurs in private, and failure in full view.

To steal ideas from one person is plagiarism; to steal from many is research.

Two wrongs are only the beginning.

Monday is an awful way to spend one-seventh of your life.

The sooner you fall behind,
the more time you'll have to catch up.

A clear conscience is usually the sign of a
bad memory.

Eagles may soar, but weasels aren't sucked
into jet engines.

When Blue Collar workers get
together, they talk about football ...

When Middle Management get
together, they talk about tennis ...

When Top Management get together,
they talk about golf.

Not from the Guinness Book of Records

Parking

Mrs Caroline Wizz (68) successfully reversed into a kerbside space of 19.36m (the equivalent of three standard parking spaces), driving an unmodified Vauxhall Nova Swing on 12 October 1993. She started the manoeuvre at 11.15 a.m. in Ropergate, Pontefract and successfully parked within three feet of the pavement 8 hours, 14 minutes later. There was slight damage to the bumpers and wings of her own and the two adjoining cars, as well as to shop frontage and two lamp-posts.

Incorrect Driving

The longest journey completed with the hand brake on was one of 313 miles from Stranraer to Hollyhead by Dr Julie Thorn at the wheel of a Saab 900 on 2 April 1987. Dr Thorn smelled burning two miles into her journey at Aird, but pressed on to Hollyhead with smoke billowing from the rear wheels. This journey also holds the record for the longest completed with the choke fully out and the right indicator flashing.

Traffic Light Cosmetics

The longest spell spent oblivious to traffic lights whilst applying make-up was one of 1 hour 15 minutes 38 seconds by Miss J. Dobson at a road junction in the centre of Preston on 1 August 1975. Miss Dobson, a piano teacher, beautified herself through 212 cycles of the traffic lights, creating a tailback of irate motorists stretching 28 miles towards Leeds.

Group Toilet Visit

The record for the largest group of women to visit a toilet simultaneously is held by 147 workers at the Department of Social Security, Longbenton, at their annual celebration at a nightclub in Newcastle upon Tyne on 12 October 1994. Mrs Beryl Crabtree got up to go to the toilet and was immediately followed by 146 other members of the party. Moving amass, the group entered the toilet at 9.52 p.m. and after waiting for everyone to finish, emerged 2 hours 37 minutes later.

Insurance claim-form gaffes compiled by the Norwich Union

✳ A Norwich Union customer collided with a cow. The questions and answers on the claim form were:

Q What warning was given by you?
A Horn.
Q What warning was given by the other party?
A Moo.

✳ I pulled into a lay-by with smoke coming from under the bonnet. I realized the car was on fire so I took my dog and smothered it with a blanket.

✳ I didn't think the speed limit applied after midnight.

✳ I was going at about 70 or 80 mph when my girlfriend on the pillion reached over and grabbed my testicles so I lost control.

✳ First car stopped suddenly, second car hit first car and a haggis ran into the rear of the second car.

✳ No witnesses would admit to having seen the mishap until after it happened.

✳ Windscreen broken. Cause unknown. Probably voodoo.

REAL PRODUCT NAMES

Sweden:
BUMS biscuits

Italy:
DRIBLY lemonade

Japan:
SKINA BABY baby lotion

Greece:
ZIT lemonade

Spain:
BONK coffee
ARSES wine

Portugal:
ATUM BOM tuna

Germany:
PLOPS savoury snacks
BUM toilet paper

France:
CRAPSY breakfast cereal
PLOPSIES breakfast cereal

Ghana:
PEE cola

Holland:
PRIK soft drink

STRANGE BUT TRUE

In America, a Wisconsin appeals judge has ruled that Guadalupe Mendoya can't sue the county for falling out of his prison cell's bed, breaking his wrist and cutting his forehead in the process – after having over 25 alcoholic drinks!

Questions That Need Answers

Do cemetery workers prefer the graveyard shift?

Actual answering machine messages

'Hi! John's answering machine is broken. This is his fridge. Please speak very slowly and I'll stick your message to myself with one of these magnets.'

'If you are a burglar, then we're at home cleaning our weapons and can't come to the phone. Otherwise we probably aren't home and it's safe to leave us a message.'

Things you don't want to overhear during surgery

'Better save that. We'll need it for the post mortem.'

'Hang on a minute, if this is his spleen, then what's that?'

'Fido, Fido, come back with that! Bad Dog!'

CLASSIFIEDS

Lost: small apricot poodle. Reward. Neutered
Like one of the family.

A superb and inexpensive restaurant.
Fine food expertly served by waitresses
in appetizing forms.

Tired of cleaning yourself? Let me do it.

3-year-old teacher needed for pre-school.
Experience preferred.

Our bikinis are exciting. They are
simply the tops.

It's tough being a guy

◆ If you put a woman on a pedestal and try to protect her from the rat race, you're a male chauvinist.

◆ If you stay at home and do the housework, you're a pansy.

◆ If you work too hard, there is never any time for her.

◆ If you don't work enough, you're a good-for-nothing bum.

◆ If you have a boring repetitive job with low pay, you should get off your butt and find something better.

◆ If you get a promotion ahead of her, that is favouritism.

◆ If she gets a job ahead of you, it's equal opportunity.

◆ If you mention how nice she looks, it's sexual harassment.

◆ If you keep quiet, it's male indifference.

◆ If you cry, you're a wimp.

◆ If you don't, you're an insensitive jerk.

◆ If you ask her to do something she doesn't enjoy, that's domination.

◆ If she asks you, it's a favour.

◆ If you try to keep yourself in shape, you're vain.

◆ If you don't you're a slob.

INTERESTING
... BUT USELESS

At one time in Holland, it took four years to train to be a hatmaker, but only three years to train to be a surgeon.

Despite the many rat-infested slums in New York City, only 311 people are bitten by rats in an average year ... but 1,519 residents are bitten annually by other New Yorkers!

No one knows why, but 90% of women who walk into a department store immediately turn to the right.

Adults average only one nightmare a year, but typically have seven sexual fantasies a day.

During his lifetime, Herman Melville's timeless classic of the sea, *Moby Dick*, only ever sold 50 copies.

Drivers tend to drive faster when other cars are around.

The world's greatest lover was King Mongut of Siam. He had 9,000 wives ... Before dying of syphilis he was quoted as saying he only loved the first 700.

Walt Disney World in Orlando, Florida, has 50,000 people on its payroll: more than the population of the average American city!

Things you only ever do in hotels

1 Pay £8 to see a film on TV.

2 Put on a posh voice when you check in.

3 Smile at people you don't know.

4 Eat shortcake biscuits.

5 Try and make the most of the 3 coat hangers in the wardrobe.

6 Press your trousers, even though they don't need pressing.

7 Carefully study all the framed adverts on the lift walls.

8 Eat a full English breakfast with 6 slices of toast.

9 Leave the bathroom tidy for when the maid comes to clean up.

10 Leave all the room lights on when you go out.

TRUE STORY

An anonymous rich bloke once played an April Fool's joke. He invited 1,000 people to a massive Ball at a big London venue.

People came from all over, not even knowing why they had been invited but just too curious not to go.

The party kicked off and everyone waited for their host to reveal himself. One hour went by, then two, while people chatted amongst themselves, drinking fabulous wine and eating canapés. Slowly the reason for them being there became clear when, as they introduced themselves to each other, they discovered that every single person there had the word 'bottom' in their surname. 'Bottomly', 'Ramsbottom', 'Hitchbottom'. There were one thousand bottoms at a party where the host never showed up.

Lost Property in Japan

The Japanese national railway has issued its annual report on items left on passenger trains. The list includes 500,000 umbrellas, £8 million in cash, 29 small dogs, one snail in a bag and 150 sets of false teeth. In addition 15 passengers left behind urns containing the ashes of dead relatives.

Women will never be equal to men until they can walk down the street bald and still think they are beautiful!

After four years' work, a psychology student on his degree paper had the question: 'What is the bravest thing you have ever done?'

He wrote, 'This is.' And left the room. He passed.

If you give a man a fish for the day, he will not go hungry. But if you teach him to fish, he'll spend the whole day in a boat drinking beer.

10 Ways To Stretch That Last Quid In Your Pocket

Buy socks all the same colour, so when one gets lost or worn out, you can still find a match.

Don't brush your teeth. Bad breath will keep people away, thus saving money on deodorant.

Trade old clothes with a friend who wears the same size and you'll get a whole new look ... free!

Keep a plastic squeeze bottle half-filled with water in the bathroom and fill it with those leftover little pieces of soap for a soap jelly that makes an efficient handwash.

Use colour comics as wrapping paper for children's gifts.

Use an old-fashioned clothespin as a 'key' for rolling up a tube of toothpaste and squeezing every last bit out of the tube.

Save the little toys and prizes you get in cereal boxes for Christmas stocking-stuffers.

Conserve water! When you shower,
stack dirty dishes at your feet.

Share 'Photo-Me' sessions … two photos
of your friend and two of you.

Hold your breath for five minutes.
(Don't try that at home, kids.)

SPOOF LOCAL NEWSPAPER HEADLINES

Body Builder Monthly
'Flatulent weightlifter accidentally drops
one on stage'

Lossiemouth Express
'Debt collector takes credit for success'

Edmonton Journal
'Grammar student has operation to
remove colon'

TRUE STORIES

■ Nike has a television commercial in America for hiking shoes that was shot in Kenya using Samburu tribesmen. The camera closes in on the one tribesman who speaks, in native Maa. As he speaks, the Nike slogan 'Just do it' appears on the screen. But Lee Cronk, an anthropologist at the University of Cincinnati, says the Kenyan is really saying, 'I don't want these. Give me *big* shoes'!

Nike's spokeswoman, Elizabeth Dolan, said, 'We didn't think anybody would know what he said!'

■ A US television station received a plea for help from a Californian resident after a report on the severe weather that the west coast had suffered which the station had attributed to El Niño.

The resident, whose name is Al Ninio, pleaded after receiving literally thousands of calls from angry strangers telling him to leave the damn weather alone. Mr Ninio claimed that he didn't know what he is supposed to have done, but that he would do anything to put it right

■ A hunter in Uganda is being sought by local authorities for illegally hunting gorillas. He shoots them with a tranquillizer gun and dresses them in clown suits. So far six gorillas have been found wandering around in this condition.

DEFINITIONS

Adult
A person who has stopped growing at both ends and is now growing in the middle.

Committee
A body that keeps minutes and wastes hours.

Egotist
Someone who is usually me-deep in conversation.

Gossip
A person who will never tell a lie if the truth will do more damage.

Secret
Something you tell to one person at a time.

Tomorrow
One of the greatest labour-saving devices of today.

Yawn
An honest opinion openly expressed.

A woman from Georgia has won $1,000 and a supply of cockroach insecticide in a contest sponsored by Combat, a company that makes bug repellent. An expert examined the woman's apartment and discovered it was infested with more than 75,000 cockroaches. The cockroaches lived in her video recorder, dishwasher, fridge, coffee-maker and oven. 'While I cook, roaches fall from the ceiling fan into my food,' the woman said.

Meanwhile in California, a man was so fed up with cockroaches roaming around his luxury apartment, that he set up eight 'bug bombs'. The explosion was so powerful that it blew out all the windows, started a fire and left the whole apartment complex with structural damage.

Politically correct terms

His jeans are not too tight;
he is Anatomically Undercirculated.

He does not get falling-down drunk;
he becomes Accidentally Horizontal.

He does not hog the duvet;
he is Thermally Unappreciative.

He is not a sex machine;
he is Romantically Automated.

He is not afraid of commitment;
he is Monogamously Challenged.

He does not have a rich daddy;
he is a Recipient of Parental Asset Infusion.

He does not have a beer gut;
he has a Liquid Grain Storage Facility.

He is not quiet;
he is a Conversational Minimalist

He is not balding;
he is in Follicle Regression.

He does not fart and belch;
he is Gastronomically Expressive.

You do not kiss him;
you become Facially Conjoined.

He is not short;
he is Anatomically Compact.

He does not eat like a pig;
he suffers from Reverse Bulimia.

REAL NEWSPAPER HEADLINES

TWO CONVICTS EVADE
NOOSE; JURY HUNG.

JUDGE TO RULE ON
NUDE BEACH.

IRAQI HEAD SEEKS ARMS.

Thin Books ...

MIKE TYSON'S GUIDE TO
DATING ETIQUETTE

DIFFERENT WAYS TO SPELL BOB

EVERYTHING MEN/WOMEN KNOW
ABOUT WOMEN/MEN

HOW TO BOIL AN EGG

BOB MONKHOUSE'S BOOK OF
FUNNY JOKES

Tips from Junior Employees to Senior Managers on how to Enhance their Relationship

Never give me work in the morning. Always wait until at least 5 p.m. – I enjoy the challenge.

If it's a really 'rush job', run in and interrupt me every 10 minutes to enquire how it's going. That helps.

Always leave without telling anyone where you are going. It gives me a chance to be creative when someone asks where you are.

If you give me more than one job to do don't tell me which one is the priority. Let me guess.

Do your best to keep me late. I like the office and really have nowhere else to go or anything to do.

If a job I do pleases you, keep it a secret. Leaks like that could win me a promotion.

If you don't like my work, tell everyone. I like my name to be popular in conversation.

If you have special instructions for a job, don't write them down. In fact, save them until a job is almost done.

Tell me all your little problems. No one else has any and it's nice to know someone is less fortunate.

Ten reasons it's great to be a guy

1 You know stuff about tanks.

2 Your ass is never a factor in a job interview.

3 All your orgasms are real.

4 You can leave a hotel bed unmade.

5 You can kill your own food.

6 You can be showered and ready in ten minutes.

7 Your underwear is £5 for a three pack.

8 Flowers fix everything.

9 Car mechanics tell you the truth.

10 You can drop by to see a friend without bringing a little gift.

SIMPLE TRUTHS

Save the whales.
Collect the whole set.

A day without sunshine is like night.

On the other hand,
you have different fingers.

Those who live by the sword get shot
by those who don't.

Despite the cost of living, have you
noticed how it remains so popular?

Recognize the inconsequential,
then ignore it.

Words of wisdom

I can please only one person per day. Today is not your day. Tomorrow isn't looking good either.

I love deadlines. I especially like the whooshing sound they make as they go flying by.

Needing someone is like needing a parachute. If he isn't there the first time you need him, chances are you won't be needing him again.

Tell me what you need, and I'll tell you how to get along without it.

Everybody is somebody else's weirdo.

Not quite true,
but should be ...

TV's consumer Watchdog, Anne Robinson, has been asked to start investigating the meat industry. Already in crisis because of the BSE scares, butchers and farmers say they need the winking wonder like a hole in the head. But Anne remains confident that she can do a fair job. 'If there's a scandal, then we'll make sure the public know about it,' she says. The first episode will concentrate on the mutton industry and will be called 'Joints of Ewe'.

Real bumper stickers

Laugh alone and the world thinks you're an idiot.

Sometimes I wake up grumpy;
other times I let her sleep.

I want to die in my sleep like my grandfather ...
Not screaming and yelling like the passengers
in his car.

The gene pool could use a little chlorine.

I didn't fight my way to the top of the food
chain to become a vegetarian.

I took an IQ test and the results were negative.

Where there's a will, I want to be in it!

If we aren't supposed to eat animals,
why are they made of meat?

He who laughs last takes too long to get the joke.

Always remember you're unique,
just like everyone else.

Ever stop to think … and forget to start again?

Jesus is coming … everyone look busy.

I said 'no' to drugs, but they just wouldn't listen.

HONG KONG MOVIE TITLES

Despite a low level of crime and violence, Hong Kong has some of the most violent martial arts movies to be seen anywhere ... and here's some of their actual film titles translated into English:

'I am damn unsatisfied to be killed in this way.'

'Fatty, you with your thick face have hurt my instep.'

'Take my advice, or I'll spank you without pants.'

'Who gave you the nerve to get killed here?'

'Quiet, or I'll blow your throat up.'

'I'll fire aimlessly if you don't come out!'

'You daring lousy guy.'

'Beat him out of recognizable shape!'

'Beware! Your bones are going to be disconnected.'

From Job Performance Evaluations

'This young lady has delusions of adequacy.'

'He would be out of his depth in a
parking lot puddle.'

'This employee is depriving a village
somewhere of an idiot.'

'He's been working with glue too much.'

'He would argue with a signpost.'

'He brings a lot of joy – whenever he
leaves the room.'

'I would not allow this employee to breed.'

'When she opens her mouth, it seems that
it is only to change feet.'

The following are actual statements found on insurance forms

As I approached an intersection a sign suddenly appeared in a place where no stop sign had ever appeared before. I was unable to stop in time to avoid the accident.

I told the police that I was not injured, but on removing my hat found that I had a fractured skull.

I was thrown from my car as it left the road. I was later found in a ditch by some stray cows.

The pedestrian ran into my car before I ran over him.

The indirect cause of the accident was a little guy in a small car with a big mouth.

The pedestrian had no idea which way to run so I ran him over.

Ten things you never hear men say …

But enough about me …

Oh, it's nothing. It's just a huge bunch of flowers I picked up on the way home.

Hi, Mum … I just called for a chat.

Let's go and see your parents this weekend.

You drive, darling, you're so much better than me.

Tell me all about your day.

No, I don't have any opinions on how the country should be run.

Isn't it your aunt's birthday tomorrow?

Oh this is delicious. I must have the recipe.

Does my new car do 0–60 in 6.5 seconds? I really hadn't noticed.

Man to God: 'God, why did you make woman so beautiful?'
God to Man: 'So you would love her.'
'But God,' Man says, 'why did you make her so dumb?'
God replies: 'So she would love you.'

Q What is the difference between men and pigs?
A Pigs don't turn into men when they drink.

These are actual excuse notes from parents to teachers (including original spelling):

✔ My son is under a doctor's care and should not take P.E. today. Please execute him.

✔ Please excuse Lisa for being absent. She was sick and I had her shot.

✔ Please excuse Gloria from Jim today. She is administrating.

✔ Please excuse Roland from P.E. for a few days. Yesterday he fell out of a tree and misplaced his hip.

✔ John has been absent because he had two teeth taken out of his face.

✔ Please excuse Jennifer for missing school yesterday. We forgot to get the Sunday paper off the porch, and when we found it Monday, we thought it was Sunday.

✔ Sally won't be in school a week from Friday. We have to attend her funeral.

OFFICE QUOTES

Quote from a recent meeting: 'We are going to continue having these meetings, every day, until I find out why no work is getting done.'

A direct quote from the Boss: 'We passed over a lot of good people to get the ones we hired.'

Quote from the Boss: 'I didn't say it was your fault. I said I was going to blame it on you.'

A motivational sign at work: 'The beatings will continue until morale improves.'

Human Resources Manager to job candidate: 'I see you've had no computer training. Although that qualifies you for upper management, it means you're under-qualified for our entry level positions.'

Quote from telephone enquiry: 'We're only hiring one summer intern this year and we won't start interviewing candidates for that position until the Boss's daughter finishes her summer classes.'

'My Boss frequently gets lost in thought. That's because it's unfamiliar territory.'

'He's given automobile accident victims new hope for recovery. He walks, talks and performs rudimentary tasks, all without the benefit of a spine.'

Creative thinking ...

A creative writing class was asked to write an essay that contained the following: religion, royalty, sex and mystery.

The prize winner read:

'My God,' said the Queen, 'I'm pregnant! I wonder who the father is?'

Ten things you never hear women say ...

I don't have any idea how many calories are in a banana.

I know it's my birthday, but I'd just like an evening in.

Please stop sending flowers to the office – it's embarrassing!

Sorry. Can't stop – no time to gossip.

Look at that new BMW move.

I'm leaving you for my secretary.

I just killed the big spider in the bathtub.

Where did you put my blue socks?

There's no need to wash those panties – I've only worn them once.

I'm so grateful to your mother for all her constructive criticism.

Occasionally, airline attendants make an effort to make the in-flight safety lecture more entertaining. Here are some real examples that have been heard or reported:

'We do feature a smoking section on this flight; if you must smoke, contact a member of the flight crew and we will escort you to the wing of the aeroplane.'

'Good morning. As we leave Dallas, it's warm, the sun is shining, and the birds are singing. We are going to Charlotte, where it's dark, windy and raining. Why in the world y'all wanna go there I really don't know.'

'Thank you for flying Delta Business Express. We hope you enjoyed giving us the business as much as we enjoyed taking you for a ride.'

'Should the cabin lose pressure, oxygen masks will drop from the overhead area. Please place the bag over your own mouth and nose before assisting children, or adults acting like children.'

'As you exit the plane, please make sure to gather all of your belongings. Anything left behind will be distributed evenly among the flight attendants. Please do not leave children or spouses.'

Things not to say to your boss

'I'm too stressed to handle this assignment.'

'Your husband/wife has a great body.'

'You must have PMS.'

'I'd sure like to get so-and-so in the broom cupboard alone.'

'I hate computers.'

'I owe a bundle to so-and-so.'

IDIOTS!

A new resident in a semi-rural area called the local township administrative office to request the removal of the 'Deer Crossing' sign on his road ... his reason was that too many deer were being hit by cars and he no longer wanted them to cross there!

An actual tip from p. 16 of the *Environment, Health & Safety Handbook for Employees*: 'Blink your eyelids periodically to lubricate your eyes.'

An employee was working particularly hard and fast one day when his boss, delighted with his efficient performance, asked him why he was working so quickly ... the employee told him that, as today was the shortest day of the year, he knew he had to work harder to get all his work done in time!

A woman in America went into her local Taco Bell, ordered a taco and asked the person behind the counter for 'minimal lettuce' … and was told 'I'm sorry, ma'am, but we only have iceberg.'

Police in Radnor, Pennsylvania, interrogated a suspect by placing a metal colander on his head and connecting it with wires to a photocopying machine. The message 'He's lying' was placed in the copier, and police pressed the copy button each time they thought the suspect was telling a lie. Believing the 'lie detector' was working, the suspect confessed.

You know you're not a kid anymore when ...

1 Your lunch box doesn't necessarily have to be a 'Star Wars' one.

2 The clothes you wear don't have your name printed on the labels.

3 You stop asking for burgers without 'bits in them'. You just take them out yourself.

4 Snow becomes a nuisance rather than fun.

5 On holiday you spend more time sunbathing than in the pool.

6 You stop saying you want to become a spaceman.

7 Puddles are something you walk around, not splash through.

8 You don't use your W.H. Smith tokens to buy CDs, but get a book.

9 Bunkbeds in the shape of a sports car are no longer cool.

10 You stay in bed later than seven-thirty.

MARRIAGE

Getting married is very much like going to a restaurant with friends. You order what you want, then when you see what the other fellow has, you wish you had ordered that.

Man is incomplete until he is married. Then he is really finished.

A little boy asked his father, 'Daddy, how much does it cost to get married?' And the father replied, 'I don't know, son, I'm still paying for it.'

'I never knew what real happiness was until I got married; and then it was too late.'

When a newly married man looks happy we know why. But when a ten-year married man looks happy – we wonder why.

A man inserted an ad in the classifieds: 'Wife wanted.' Next day he received hundreds of letters. They all said the same thing: 'You can have mine.'

When a man opens the door of his car for his wife you can be sure of one thing: either the car is new, or his wife is.

The following are the top three winners of a Most Embarrassing Moments Contest in *New Woman* magazine

1

While in line at the bank one afternoon, my toddler decided to release some pent-up energy and ran amok. I was finally able to grab hold of her after receiving looks of disgust and annoyance from other patrons and I told her that if she did not start behaving 'right now' she would be punished. To my horror, she looked me in the eye and said in a voice just as threatening. 'If you don't let me go right now, I will tell Grandma that I saw you kissing Daddy's pee-pee last night!'

2

It was the day before my eighteenth birthday. I was living at home, but my parents had gone out for the evening, so I invited my girlfriend over for a romantic night alone. As we lay in bed after making love, we heard the telephone ring downstairs. For a bit of fun I decided to give my girlfriend a piggyback ride to the phone, but as I didn't want to miss the call, we didn't

bother getting dressed. When we got to the bottom of the stairs, the lights suddenly came on and a whole crowd of people yelled, 'Surprise!' … My entire family – aunts, uncles, grandparents, cousins – and all my friends were standing there for my surprise birthday party!

3

A lady picked up several items at a discount store but when she got up to the till, she realized that one of her items had no price tag. Imagine her embarrassment when the checker got on the intercom and boomed out for all the store to hear: 'Price check on Tampax supersize, please.' That was bad enough, but somebody at the rear of the store apparently misunderstood the word 'tampax' for 'thumbtacks' and, in a business-like tone, a voice boomed back over the intercom: 'Do you want the kind you push in with your thumb or the kind you pound in with a hammer?'

Some oxymorons

Tight slacks

Pretty ugly

Diet ice cream

Working vacation

Alone together

Silent scream

Exact estimate

Found missing

Good grief

Living dead

Small crowd

Act naturally

Clearly misunderstood

Peace force

Plastic glasses

Women's snappy comebacks to pickup lines ...

Man: Haven't I seen you someplace before?
Woman: Yeah, that's why I don't go there anymore.

Man: I know how to please a woman.
Woman: Then please leave me alone.

Man: So what do you do for a living?
Woman: I'm a female impersonator.

Man: Hey, come on, we're both here at this bar for the same reason.
Woman: Yeah! Let's pick up some chicks.

Man: I would go to the end of the world for you.
Woman: Yes, but would you stay there?

TRUE STORIES

✦ Police in Oakland spent two hours attempting to subdue a gunman who had barricaded himself inside his home. After firing ten tear gas canisters, officers discovered that the man was standing beside them, shouting pleas to come out and give himself up ...

✦ An Illinois man pretending to have a gun kidnapped a motorist and forced him to drive to two different automated teller machines. The kidnapper then proceeded to withdraw money from his own bank accounts ...

✦ Fire investigators on Maui have determined the cause of a blaze that destroyed a $127,000 home recently – a short in the homeowner's newly installed fire prevention alarm system. 'This is even worse than last year,' said the distraught homeowner, 'when someone broke in and stole my new security system ...'

✦ In Ohio, an unidentified man in his late twenties walked into a police station with a nine-inch wire protruding from his forehead and calmly asked officers to give him an X-ray to help him find his

brain, which he claimed had been stolen. Police were shocked to learn that the man had drilled a six-inch deep hole in his skull with a Black & Decker power drill and had stuck the wire in to try and find the missing brain!

✦ Police in Los Angeles had good luck with a robbery suspect who just couldn't control himself during a line-up. When detectives asked each man in the line-up to repeat the words, 'Give me all your money or I'll shoot,' the man shouted, 'That's not what I said!'

✦ In Modesto, Steven Richard King was arrested for trying to hold up a Bank of America branch without a weapon. King used a thumb and a finger to simulate a gun, but unfortunately, he failed to keep his hand in his pocket.

✦ A man spoke frantically into the phone: 'My wife is pregnant and her contractions are only two minutes apart!'
'Is this her first child,' the doctor asked.
'No, you idiot,' the man shouted. 'This is her husband!'

Bizarre interview behaviour, taken from the *Washington Post*

★ A candidate stretched on the floor to fill out the job application.

★ Interviewee wore a Walkman and said she could listen to me and the music at the same time.

★ Applicant challenged interviewer to arm wrestle.

★ Said if he were hired, he would demonstrate his loyalty by having the corporate logo tattooed to his forearm.

★ Interrupted to phone his therapist for advice on answering specific interview questions.

★ Wouldn't get out of the chair until I agreed to hire him. I had to call the police.

★ Took a brush out of her purse and brushed her hair.

★ Pulled out a Polaroid camera and snapped a flash picture of me. Said he collected photos of everyone who interviewed him.

★ Asked who the lovely babe was, pointing to the picture on my desk. When I said it was my wife, he asked if she was now home and wanted my phone number. I called security.

From a medical dictionary ...

Antibody – against everyone

Bacteria – back door to a cafeteria

Benign – what you be after you be eight

Cardiology – advanced study of poker playing

Cauterize – made eye contact with her

Congenital – friendly

Dilate – to live longer

Impotent – distinguished, well known

Labour pain – hurt at work

Paralyse – two far-fetched stories

Protein – in favour of young people

Tablet – a small table

Tumour – an extra pair

Urine – opposite of 'you're out'

Vein – conceited

CHAT-UP LINES

*'If I could rearrange the alphabet,
I'd put "U" and "I" together.'*

'That dress would look great on the floor next to my bed!'

*'Do you have ten pence … because I need to call my mother
and tell her I just found the woman of my dreams!'*

*'Are you religious? … Good.
Because I'm the answer to your prayers.'*

'Would you like to see me naked?'

DID YOU KNOW ...

There are more Japanese banks in London than Tokyo.

Snails can sleep for up to three years without waking up.

There are more Irish people in New York than Dublin.

£1 notes stopped being legal currency in England in 1988 but there are still 57 million of them in circulation.

You can now buy gravestones which include an imbedded 5-by-4-inch video screen which can show highlights of your life. They're priced around £4,000.

A lead pencil could draw a line 35 miles long.

After the first, birthdays are celebrated
every ten years in China.

Golf balls used to be made with honey
inside them.

It very rarely snows in Antarctica.

The Ancient Egyptians trained baboons to
wait on tables.

Taxi drivers in Nottingham have to keep
a bale of hay in their boot.

The frankfurter originated in China.

Gone With the Wind was originally called
Ba Ba Black Sheep.

In Egypt people greet each other by saying,
'How do you sweat?'

One night, a Delta twin-engine puddle jumper was flying somewhere above America. There were five people on board: the pilot, Michael Jordan, Bill Gates, the Dalai Lama, and a hippie. Suddenly there was a loud explosion and the plane began to fill with smoke …

The pilots tells the passengers, 'I have some good news and some bad news. The bad news is that we're about to crash in New Jersey. The good news is that there are four parachutes, and I have one of them!' With that he opened the door and jumped out of the aeroplane.

Michael Jordan was on his feet in a flash. 'Gentlemen,' he said, 'I am the world's greatest athlete. The world needs great athletes. I think I should have a parachute!' With these words, he grabbed a parachute and hurtled through the door into the night.

Bill Gates rose and said, 'Gentlemen, I am the world's smartest man. The world needs smart men. I think the world's smartest man should have a parachute.' He grabbed one, and out he jumped.

The Dalai Lama and the hippie looked at one another. Finally, the Dalai Lama spoke. 'My son,' he said, 'I have lived a satisfying life and have known the bliss of True Enlightenment. You have your life ahead of you; you take the last parachute, and I will go down with the plane.'

The hippie smiled and said, 'Hey, don't worry. The world's smartest man just jumped out wearing my backpack.'

*A magazine recently ran a 'Dilbert Quotes' contest.
It was looking for people to submit quotes from their
real-life Dilbert-type managers.
Here are some of the submissions:*

❖ As of tomorrow, employees will only be able to
   access the building using individual security cards.
   Employees will receive their cards in two weeks.

❖ What I need is a list of specific unknown problems
   we will encounter.

❖ E-mail is not to be used to pass on information or
   data. It should be used only for company business.

❖ This project is so important, we can't let things that
   are more important interfere with it.

❖ No one will believe you solved this problem in one
   day! We've been working on it for months. Now,
   go act busy for a few weeks and I'll let you know
   when it's time to tell them.

❖ We know that communication is a problem, but
   the company is not going to discuss it with the
   employees.

English signs in foreign countries

In a Japanese hotel
You are invited to take advantage of the chambermaid.

At a Budapest zoo
Please do not feed the animals. If you have any suitable food, give it to the guard on duty.

In the office of a Romanian doctor
Specialist in women and other diseases.

In a Zurich hotel
'Because of the impropriety of entertaining guests of the opposite sex in the bedroom, it is suggested that the lobby be used for this purpose.'

In a Norwegian cocktail lounge
'Ladies are requested not to have children in the bar.'

ACTUAL NEWSPAPER HEADLINES

SOMETHING WENT WRONG IN
JET CRASH, EXPERT SAYS.

POLICE BEGIN CAMPAIGN TO
RUN DOWN JAYWALKERS.

SAFETY EXPERTS SAY SCHOOL BUS
PASSENGERS SHOULD BE BELTED.

DRUNK GETS NINE MONTHS
IN VIOLIN CASE.

PROSTITUTES APPEAL TO POPE.

MINERS REFUSE TO WORK
AFTER DEATH.

SHOT OFF WOMAN'S LEG HELPS
NICKLAUS TO 66.

ENRAGED COW INJURES FARMER
WITH AXE.

STOLEN PAINTING FOUND BY TREE.

CHEF THROWS HIS HEART INTO
HELPING FEED NEEDY.

KIDS MAKE NUTRITIOUS SNACKS.

IF STRIKE ISN'T SETTLED QUICKLY
IT MAY LAST A WHILE.

TYPHOON RIPS THROUGH CEMETERY.
HUNDREDS DEAD.

TWO SOVIET SHIPS COLLIDE, ONE DIES.

RED TAPE HOLDS UP NEW BRIDGE.

MAN MINUS EAR WAIVES HEARING.

PROSECUTOR RELEASES PROBE
INTO UNDERSHERIFF.

World Cup commentary blinders

'The Croatians don't play well without the ball.'

Barry Venison

'Batistuta gets most of his goals with the ball.'

Ian St John

'The good news for Nigeria is that they're two-nil down very early in the game.'

Kevin Keegan

'I wouldn't be surprised if this game went all the way to the finish.'

Ian St John

'Apart from their goals, Norway haven't scored.'

Terry Venables

'Pires has got something about him, he can go both ways depending on who's facing him.'

David Pleat

'Chile have three options – they could win or they could lose.'

Kevin Keegan

'Strangely, in slow motion replay, the ball seemed to hang in the air for even longer.'

David Acfield

'I came to Nantes two years ago and it's much the same today, except that it's completely different.'

Kevin Keegan

'He dribbles a lot and the opposition don't like it - you can see it all over their faces.'

Big Ron

'If we played like that every week we wouldn't be so inconsistent.'

Bryan Robson, Manchester United

'I spent a lot of my money on booze, birds and fast cars. The rest I just squandered.'

George Best

'There's nobody fitter at his age, except maybe Raquel Welch.'

Ron Atkinson lauds Gordon Strachan, 39